The Keys To Light
By: Keybearer

© 2009 By Keybearer

ISBN: 978-0-578-01561-3

Disclaimer: Self Injury is a serious disorder. Please seek out properly trained medical and mental health professionals. I assume no liability for the use of any suggestions or insights contained in this book.

---Keybearer

Dedication:

To Hecate, thank you isn't enough. I only hope I prove worthy for whatever you ask of me in the future.

To my teacher, above and beyond you truly went and there are no words to describe my gratitude. I only hope I can be half as good as I move out along my path. Best wishes along your path wherever it may lead you.

To John, Dr. Debarthe, and JT, the support of each of you set the stage and is not forgotten.

To all the others whose paths have touched mine, and who have supported me in ways both big and small, Thank You!

Table of Contents

Chapter	Title	Page
Prologue	Prologue	5
1	The Fall To Darkness	6
2	A Shiny Silver Friend	11
3	A Bare Glimmer Of Light	13
4	Daring To Believe	15
5	Time of Transition	19
6	Hecate Enters	24
7	Falling…But Light	27
8	Introducing Hecate	30
9	At The Crossroads	33
10	The Seeds Of Doubt	35
11	Changing Identities	38
12	Other Divine Assistance	40
13	Beginning To Move On	45
14	Who I Am	49
15	The Mundane Influence	52
16	Now To The Present	54
17	Thru The Darkness To Light	59
Bibliography	Bibliography	61

Prologue

"In our darkness lies our greatest strength." It is both a lesson and also my personal motto I've come to live my life by, as I've journeyed with the dark Goddess from depression and self injury to a life of friendships, safety and hope.

The dark Goddess is feared and yet she is also widely respected. She is feared for her ability to drive one to madness by bringing up things we would much rather avoid. In pagan cosmology it is known and understood that life and death are two sides of the same coin. One can not exist without the other. Yet the Goddess in her dark aspect is feared and those who embrace her are at times feared as well. Why? I think, because the lessons she teaches are amongst the hardest and she allows no excuses. She dredges up our deepest fears buried deep into our souls such that we've forgotten them and gives them a name, a face. We have no choice but to face them and learn their lessons. The alternate is madness as our psyche comes apart under the strain. Yet, properly embraced she can provide for the deepest healings The story I'm about to tell is a journey into the dark side of my psyche, of meeting the dark Goddess, accepting her and walking with her back into the light. It is the story of finding my true self.

Perhaps my story will encourage another to find the courage to accept the dark Goddess, embrace and walk with her on their own journey to healing.

Chapter 1: The Fall To Darkness

To understand my journey and the work I've done with the Goddess herself, I first must tell you of my beginnings and my fall into darkness.

I was born August 16, 1975. I remember nearly nothing of my childhood before my eleventh birthday, and the memories from that point on are not pleasant. I have been told I was premature, sickly and that the doctors had told my parents to put me in an institution. That I'd never walk, or talk. I was told I had severe seizures and remember taking many medications. The summer of my eleventh birthday I spent in a full body cast after leg surgeries. It was summer and the cast was hot, itchy, and smelly. I had no friends except one, but she only visited a couple of times. She stopped after my mother yelled at her for getting me some ice from the freezer. Imagine a very lonely child now cut off from all friends. My parents thought they were doing right by me, but it was to prove to be the beginning of the end for me. It marked the start of a dive into the depths of darkness and depression that left my mind, body and soul a disjointed phantom of what it was meant to be.

That fall I entered middle school, and my parents thinking I'd still be in a wheelchair had arranged for me to be in a small homeroom. I was placed in with four or five other students all of which were hearing impaired. I didn't fit in with them, nor could I relate to any of the kids in my other classes. I'd spent much of my childhood alone and lacked the skills to really relate to and make friends of the other children. I kept to myself preferring the company of adults to those my own age and preferring most of all to be alone. I was on crutches for awhile and how the doctor had me using them had the other children thinking I didn't really need them and this was the starting point for the teasing. Kids are cruel and have no understanding of the true power of the words they say, let alone their actions. I dealt with the name calling, the isolation and the throwing of gum and paper. No one stopped them, no one held them accountable, and voicing my pain to my family just brought more pain on to me.

Even when it got so bad that I came home from school and had to have gum cut from my clothes, when it went down a back brace I was in, it was still my fault. A back brace worn to straighten a spine that abuse and depression was bending. "Stand up straight" my father would say to me and we fought about it constantly. People don't understand that most communication is done by physical gestures and postures. Standing up straight denotes self esteem and confidence which I had little of and what little I had was being eroded little by little. My parent's comments bit deep. "If you'd stand straighter, dress nicer…etc…they'd like you more." No matter how hard I tried I couldn't seem to improve things and soon I stopped trying. School got worse over time. Eventually, things got so bad I couldn't even cross paths with other kids on the street with out more abuse.

By high school the only friend I had was my dog and each day I took her to a local park. One fall day while we were there we encountered some boys from school. They called my name and when I looked up they threw a tomato hitting me in the chest. They walked away laughing. Inside I wondered, why does everyone hate me? Why doesn't anyone care enough to make them stop? A portion of my soul cried that day, but my body merely laid its head down on my dogs back. I was to deeply depressed to do anything more. I was living in blackness so deep that even the sun could not penetrate. I'd already begun self injuring using the wounds on my body to control the hurt no one would hear, to keep my emotions in balance and to give myself something in my life I could control. I was in a black pit where I no longer mattered. I rarely spoke, I didn't make eye contact, and my grades had slipped. The only thing that mattered was my dog and my razor, and with good reason. There is nothing more loyal then a dog and an inanimate object. They were my only safety. Yes, even the razor was safe even as it was slowly taking away more and more of my ability to cope. I didn't hide the bandages at school, yet no one noticed. Here's a child desperate, scared with ace bandages or, gauze and tape around her wrist most days and yet no one noticed. Not even the counselor whose office I sat in each day at lunch. I was a child falling thru the cracks, a child whose very soul is withering and barely clinging to life, to reality, and yet no one notices.

One may question that just because school was bad was that really reason enough to start hurting yourself, to start cutting and eventually burning your own body? Alone probably not but, you see as bad as school was, home was worse. At the end of the school day when I should have felt relief, I shivered with fear at what I might encounter at home. A mother who was both, violently bipolar and a severely brittle diabetic, a father submissive and withdrawn. Life was ruled by my mother's moods and illnesses. The littlest of things could set her off. The simplest of disagreements with my father would turn into weeks of her living in the basement in near darkness. Eventually she'd stop talking to each member of the family in turn, stop taking her medications and even at times start drinking. The result is that she would end up violently ill and dehydrated nearly to the point of becoming unconscious. There were times of violence. I'd be sitting in my room reading and she'd barge in and start screaming inches from my face "If you can't be a proper daughter, then you're not my daughter at all!" She left nasty notes around the house for my father even at times placing them on his forehead. At times she'd throw out food and clothes. She often would have my brother or I take her to an ATM where she would pull out hundreds of dollars and never tell my father. I soon learned to mention these episodes and the worry was always, will the mortgage check clear? It was a constant worry on his part. The constant worry on my part was, "Is today the day I come home and find her dead?" "Will it be from dehydration, Diabetes or at her own hand?" The ending to each episode took one of two forms, either she became so ill I called an ambulance or so violent I called the police.

The first night I called the police I was in high school. I'd come home late one evening from a boyfriend's birthday party. The peace of 1a.m. was shattered by the lights shining in my parents' bedroom window. The lights alone were enough to warn me of the troubles inside the house. Walking in I could hear her smacking him, but this night I'd had enough. Walking into their room the child who should have been protected became the adult doing the protecting. "That is enough!" "If you hit him one more time I'm calling the police." "Go ahead they will just make you leave" She responded. "I don't think so because I'm reporting this as spousal abuse." I called 911 and I heard the click, click of scissors. I knew what she was doing but I had no intention of stopping her. She came in and pulled the phone from the wall, which I calmly reported to the dispatcher as she did it thus disconnecting us. She left the room and I heard the sound of a knife thru skin. If you've never heard it, it sounds similar to a knife thru cucumber. I'd had enough, if she was going to kill herself I was prepared to let her. My father was still lying in bed and the only words I spoke to him were, "I'm sorry but this can not go on." I left the house and sat down on the porch. After a few minutes I went in to find her holding a knife, pinned against the kitchen counter, my father holding her arms. There was blood all over the carpet and walls. My father instructed me to call an ambulance. I ran to a neighbor's who happened to be awake and he placed the call. I left and returned to my home as the police and ambulance arrived. Inside my mother in her deranged state was telling the police how my father likes his bath water. The rest of the night my father and I spent scrubbing the blood from the walls and carpet. To be alone with the thoughts and fears this incident and others generated, to have no place of respite, is a lot for anyone. But for a child struggling with their own depression, their own self worth it was all that much harder. I learned no one would protect me, no one will believe me. I learned that I'm different from other kids and that my best isn't good enough. I learned that I don't walk, talk, or even dress myself right. And most importantly I learned I could trust no one. These lessons were nearly fatal.

People fear death. They spend billions of dollars each year trying to look younger or stave off death. I believe however, that there are fates worse then death. The death of hope, the death of laughter, the death of ones ability to feel and the death of spirit, are all far worse than the death of the physical body.

My depression had started with the tensions in school, during middle school and by high school was deeply engrained. At this point I started what was to be a long, loving yet destructive relationship with self injury.

Chapter 2: A Shiny Silver Friend

While a freshman in high school, I had taken on a job volunteering in the library before classes each morning and I enjoyed it. My sophomore year, I had encouraged someone I'd thought was a friend to work there as well. At the end of the preceding summer I'd taken this friend to my grandparents for a weekend visit. The neighbors were down with their kids and by the end of the weekend they were following my friend's lead in everything and had exchanged phone numbers and addresses, information that they had never shared with me. Angry at being tossed aside, I got the address of the one girl from my Grandmother, and wrote to her about it. She wrote back and her words, lost now to my memory, left me feeling lied to. In school I watched my friend excel at making friends, at our work in the library, at her classes. The black wave of loneliness, depression, hopelessness and self loathing that had been following me and building for so many years, finally broke over me. I was sitting in the back room of the library alone and I looked down at my wrist…"I HATE YOU!" I said as I tore at my wrist with my nails until I left a wound. The relief I felt was instant. It was as if a huge boulder was lifted off my shoulders and I was calm, even in part in awe of the power I'd just wielded over myself. The scratching became wrist banging and all the bandages went unnoticed. The one time it was noticed by a librarian she jokingly asked "Should we search you for razors?" I replied "Maybe you should and walked away." Nothing more was said to me about it by anyone. I learned years later that one librarian had said something to my guidance counselor, yet nothing had ever been done. Again, the lesson was driven home, no one cares about you. The counselor saw me each day at lunch, heard the stories, yet still was blind and deaf to a child in trouble. The wrist banging led to razor cutting. The first cuts were hardly worse then scratches, but over time progressed to more, more often and deeper. Things at home remained violent and unpredictable, things at school and on the street also unsafe. I learned that the razor would numb the pain and I would be able to not feel for awhile. I learned that sometimes when I was tired of being numb I could cut and feel for a time. I could prove my existence by the sight of the blood seeping from my cut skin. I would write the words of my own self loathing in my blood upon my body…freak, lonely, stupid, failure, ugly, useless, trash, die…words that spoke the truth of a soul that was dying. A soul that wanted nothing more than to be friendly, and to be with animals and to read was beaten down to the point where nothing mattered but my animals and a shiny silver razor. I'd leaned to avoid people at all costs, and I avoided eye contact at all costs. At home I stayed in my room with the door shut alone. I leaned that animals would be the only thing that wouldn't hurt me. My books were a desperate escape from fear and loneliness, and boredom. The razors were my control, the only thing I could control. I had become little more than a whisper of a shadow of the person I could have been. I had become cut off from my feelings and numb to nearly everything.

Chapter 3: A Bare Glimmer of Light

I started at a community college the fall after my high school graduation, my grades far to poor for anything else. I was in danger of failing out my first semester and my father's words bit deep. "Drop out if you want to." He never even tried to urge me to keep going. My response was "No.". All my life the animals had been my only friends, my knowledge of them was the only thing I'd ever been given credit for. In the depths of my being I had always known that they would be my way out. I continued with school, but I also continued to self injure.

A fight with my boyfriend ended me up in the emergency room for evaluation. I was released to a counselor at the college but I didn't go at first. Looking back, I can see the hand of the Goddess at work even here, for it really was chancy on the part of the social worker that evaluated me to have released me. I would learn later this social worker knew and worked closely with the counselor she had referred me to. A couple of months later a classmate turned me on to the same counselor. The lady has no issues with repeating herself if we don't get it the first time thru.

Desperate, alone, and increasingly suicidal I finally went to see him. He was the first person to finally take me seriously about the situation and to tell me it wasn't my fault. I saw him daily for about six months venting and finally for the first time, being heard. Yet I continued to self injure and the severity was increasing. Desperate one day I said to him "My mother is not the only one suicidal." "Who else?" He asked. In that fateful moment I told him of the self injury and of feeling suicidal. He promptly arranged for me to be seen at a local clinic. It was the beginning of a string of therapists, each as clueless as the one before. I was asked questions I could not answer, either because I lacked the knowledge, the words, the ability to articulate or even identify feelings and states of mind. To say the least I found them to be less than helpful. I've had therapists sit and stare at me in silence. I had one apologize for not believing me about how my father would be. I even had one fall asleep on the moments after I said to him "There is so much inside and I can't get it out." His response was "o.k.". The only friend I had at this point was the counselor back at the college. My family remained unstable and violent, and my grades continued to be poor. I was clinging to home and life by a thread and now the professionals were failing me time after time. My razor remained a valued friend. Somehow I earned my A.A. degree and in so doing opened a back door into the University of Maryland. My grades alone would never have gotten me in but there was an agreement with Maryland that if the most recent coursework was an associate's degree acceptance was guaranteed. The transition meant going someplace where I knew no one and had no support. But my time with the counselor at the community college had served its purpose. It allowed me to dare to think that maybe, just maybe it wasn't my fault and someone really would listen. My self injury continued however and it was continuing to grow worse.

Chapter 4: Daring to Believe

My Time at Maryland was turbulent to say the least. I failed out and gained reinstatement three times. I knew no one there and my family remained in turmoil. Amidst it all my mother was diagnosed with cancer. I owe my eventual success at Maryland to a professor, the farm manager and a flock of sheep.

The professor was also my advisor and in time he became a friend. Dr. Jerry Debarthe was well loved and respected by faculty, staff, and students alike. Everyone knew if you needed help he would give it. Meeting with him often ended with hugs, big warm protective bear hugs that brought a smile to even the saddest of faces. One day in class he noticed bandages on both my wrists and with motions to his own he questioned me. I shook my head no and he left it be. Again I was desperate and alone, so I decided to confide in him. I had nothing left to lose. Up in his office he brought his chair around his desk to sit facing me without a barrier between us. It was a gesture of respect and attention, and it meant a great deal. We ended that day and as I turned to leave he asked me, "Could you use a hug?". In that moment he provided more relief then he knew. I responded yes with my voice, but my body screamed it. My head came up, and my shoulders dropped. Words can lie but touch can not. He never stopped supporting and encouraging me. He even told me how to change my major to satisfy the university's requirement for reinstatement and yet still let me take the courses for my degree. His death from a heart attack only a year and a half after meeting him was a huge loss to me. Even to this day I wonder what he would say about various things and I sure do miss those hugs! After an animal handling lab, he gained permission from our farm manager to allow us to go up and visit the new lambs. An animal lover I'd always been and it was love at first sight. Over time I began to spend more time around the farm and in particular with the sheep, a powerful protective totem in their own right and totally appropriate for where I was at the time.

My second semester on campus I was about to begin my anatomy course which required the purchase of a dissection kit complete with scalpel blades. My relationship with my razor and my self injury was still ongoing and yet I desperately wanted to be free of it. I needed it yet I knew that it was destroying me. The straight razor was sharp the scalpel blade far more so and I feared what I could do to myself with it. Alone, depressed, and frightened I did what I'd always done, I sought out the animals for support. I wandered down to the farm, late one evening and found the farm deserted. I spent my time visiting with the horses. In retrospect it is interesting to have been with the horses as they represent movement and freedom. The farm manager arrived to check the lambs and expectant ewes and on his way back out he greeted me and asked "How's it going?" I responded "I've been better." "What's going on?" I confided my struggles and my fears as he walked me back to my dorm. He offered to keep the kit between classes for me and I accepted. Over time he became a much trusted friend and teacher. He learned more and more about me and saw me at both my best and worst. He provided support, encouragement and many swift kicks in the ass along the way. There were rules, for the most part simple, but for me they were a struggle. Look up, make eye contact, keep up at feeding, stay away between certain times, and speak up. Simple things, but for one terrified of people and with self esteem lower than low they were as huge a challenge as climbing Everest. Yet he encouraged the littlest of improvement. I had the privilege of spending my time outside of class with the sheep sitting, petting, keeping watch on the expectant ewes, and bottle feeding the orphans. My time with them was the bright spot that helped me endure.

Over time with the support of the sheep and their shepherd I began to ever so slowly peep out of my shell and associate more and more with those around me. I was far from well however, and the injuring continued and the suicidal feelings as well. The most serious injury I ever inflicted on myself, occurred in the living room of the house I was living in at the time. I don't remember now what had triggered me. I remember only being numb and out of it cutting my wrist. Everything around me was surreal, fuzzy and distant. When I came back to myself, back to reality, I realized the tendons in my wrist were exposed and that I'd been trying to cut them as well. This was the first time I truly got scared. I realized how completely disconnected I'd been during the process. Frightened though I was the internal terror and hopelessness I felt was far worse and opening my wrist became the new standard for my self injury. Eventually the repeated cutting of the same spot caused an overgrowth of tissue that itched and wept. The campus health center had no idea what it was. One nurse in what I assume was an attempt to help asked me if I realized I could lose my hand. I said yes. I was frightened but not enough to stop. Self injury was still the only way I knew to cope with my internal states. The health center referred me to a surgeon thinking that I might need surgery to remove the extra tissue. When I told the surgeon what had happened he asked me what self injury was. Telling him was a mistake as his whole attitude towards me changed and he began to treat me as if I was merely a bother. I knew that the self injury I had been using to cope and survive had taken over and I was out of control. I knew I was moving along a path that would end me up dead, emotionally or physically. Though I had tried suicide several times, deep down all I truly wanted was to fit in, for the fear and pain to stop, and to understand why I was and always had been different. Answers were coming but had not yet arrived.

When I hit the point of trying to hang myself it was because I'd lost all hope of things getting better. I was overwhelmed to the point that even the self injury wasn't working. While I was in the hospital, the farm manager called and allowed me to call him. I spoke more to him while I was in the hospital then I did to my family. The look in his eyes when he first found out what I'd done somehow made me realize that for once someone really cared what happened and maybe, just maybe, he was for real and not acting out of cultural expectations. That realization planted a seed for healing, that would slowly germinate and grow to allow me to begin the process of recovery, but it would take much time

In the darkness of the night

with the pressure of the day behind

behind but not forgotten

not forgotten, or gone

desire rears it's ugly head for silver steel

or red hot flame

red or yellow relief, which will it be?

But, mixed in the sea of emotion a desire to stop.

The agony and the dark relief,

which will win this night?

red or yellow or respect for the soul?

No one can be sure, no one ever knows.

And so, night after night week after

Week,

year after lonely year.

The endless struggle rages on,

When will it end? 10/3/01

Chapter 5: Time of Transition

Time passed slowly. I began to socialize with the other students and make friends. Yet I was never truly able to feel accepted or good enough. My mother died half way thru college. I received the call late one night during finals week that there was nothing more that the doctors could do. She crossed over on August 9, 1998. I have to give Hospice of Baltimore the highest of praise for their care not only of her but of her family and friends. My father spent most of his free time at her bedside and as her time grew short so did my siblings. My father felt that I should speak to her, though what he thought I should say I wasn't clear. I had nothing I wanted to say to her. What could I say to a woman who had given me so many bad memories, so much pain? All I felt was hate towards her and it was a relief when she got too ill to play her games, to yell and to scream anymore. I was there when she passed. My brother called me at home early that Sunday morning and I headed to the hospice. I arrived just in time to kiss her goodbye. My last words to her were "Bye Mom" with a kiss. All I felt was relief. All the sympathy, the "I'm so sorry" from family and friends drove me nuts. Sorry for what? Sorry that the games and terror were over? Sorry that the revolving door trips to the emergency room were over? In truth her Diabetes had been so severe, so out of control and was causing her so many other problems that the cancer may well have been a blessing. She was gone but the damage she inflicted remained and I continued to self injure and struggle. It would be several years before I would resolve my issues with her and begin to appreciate all the good she had done for me.

My injuries continued to be increasingly severe and yet my grades were beginning to improve. I Went from less then a 2.0 in my starting semesters to over 3.0 with a semester high of 3.76. My grades were an indicator of the slow path to healing I had embarked on. I graduated in December 2000. I had no job lined up or real plans. How could I, I'd spent most of my energies staying alive, not really expecting to make it thru. My first job was on a dairy farm in Pennsylvania. The move left me homesick, the work, exhausted, and with a case of carpal tunnel. Still injuring and depressed my job lasted barely a month, before I moved home. I then took a job in a stable at a private school. This job too went poorly. The work itself wasn't hard, but when all of one's energy is focused on breathing in each moment, all other things are just not that important. This job lasted about four months, but the winds of change and healing had begun to pick up strength. The hands of the Goddess were at work, though it would be more than another year before she would introduce herself to me.

During my times at Maryland I had come across a book titled Bodily Harm. It talked about self injury and described a treatment program specifically for it called Safe Alternatives. I read the book and cried all the way thru it. It was the first contact I'd had with anyone that understood. I had had numerous therapists and none had understood or been helpful. I remember driving home from campus one day, feeling frustrated, having tried to locate someone local with a clue and having failed, and also after having tried to get into the program before and failed. Here I was with a lead on a program that understood how I was feeling yet I was unable to get there. I was getting worse, the urges stronger and more frequent, and the injuries more severe. The cutting had given way to second degree burns. I remember driving home and saying out loud "I don't know when or how but I WILL go to Safe." Magic works. In the losing of this job it manifested.

I realized that I had enough money for one month of cobra coverage, and I now had the free time. I made the call to the program and started the admission process. They were willing to admit me. There were two catches however, the first was that I needed to come up with over two thousand dollars up front, the expected co-pay after insurance, and the second that I would have to fly out and then after I arrived have the intake person call my insurance company for final approval. There was no guarantee that I would get in. How bad did I want this? I had no choice but to speak to my father and ask for the money to go. He seemed shocked and more then a little taken aback when he found out. I suppose a fair reaction to finding out your daughter is injuring her body. For me this was the hardest part of the process. In the end he agreed to give me the money. I arrived at SAFE on February 18, 2002. The insurance company gave me their approval and I began thirty days of group sessions, writing assignments, and personal therapy. Thirty days of realizing it wasn't my fault and it had not only been as bad as I thought, but worse. During this time my father admitted that my mother had chased him around the house with a knife. "Dad, why didn't you get us out of there?" His answer shocked both me and my counselor to silence. "Because I never thought she'd hurt you kids." Thirty days to realize that I was o.k., and that my family was crazy in their functioning. Thirty days to realize that I believed my father would like someone else as a daughter. Any illusion I'd had of my relationship with my father being better than with my mother shattered in that moment. By the end of the thirty days I was beginning to see truly how crazy my situation had been. I began to realize that I was o.k., and that I have a right to my thoughts and feelings. I was afraid to return home since I knew nothing with my father had changed and I was concerned that being back in the situation would set me back. One of the therapists however pointed out that while my father had not changed I had.

I returned home, March 20th. My regular therapist at home still seemed to have no clue and the one after him didn't either. In fact I was told to try things when I was triggered that were completely counter to what I learned at SAFE. Eventually I gave up on therapy, for to try working with someone telling me counter to what I'd learned and found helpful was doing more harm than good. I'd been on various medications over the years and had always had a hard time handling them as they increased the number of migraines I had.

The doctors always told me they would pass as I adjusted to the medicines, but they never did. Can you imagine a migraine for days let alone weeks? I invariably would stop the medications as a result. Self Injury is an issue of feelings, thoughts, communication, and self-esteem and as such I have issues with the idea of long term medications for its treatment. But we live in a society of "quick fixes" and instant gratification. We live in a society where feeling bad is a negative instead of a normal part of life and a symptom of the real issues. Just before SAFE and during my stay I was once again placed on meds, this time however, when I complained of the migraines I was given something to relieve them. That was enough to encourage me to be willing to stay on them. A few months after coming home from SAFE, with no insurance, not working and with the growing awareness that my therapist and doctor were viewing the medications as permanent I stopped them and shortly after the therapy as well. I managed seven moths and a day safe before I relapsed.

Despite the relapse something had changed. Instead of sitting at home, I was out and about, I was looking for work and I knew that I didn't want to be as before. That whole summer I was increasingly restless for reasons I could not identify. I was pacing the floors, and not sleeping. I had said to the farm manager, who remained a friend "I feel like I'm supposed to be someplace doing something but I don't know what." My answer came one day when I decided to go to the movies to try to distract myself and calm down. With time to kill before the show I wandered into Barnes and Noble. An avid reader my whole life this wasn't a surprise, the book I picked up however, was different than any I'd read before and was the catalyst that would change my life, introduce me to the dark Goddess and allow me to heal. The book was called Simply Wicca. The path it placed me on was and is anything but simple, but I'm all the better for it. It is an unassuming looking purple book, but when I looked at it on the display table it seemed to glow. I'd only heard of Wicca in passing thru someone I was chatting with online. I was curious and being that I enjoy learning I decided to give it a read. Besides, how often do you see a book glow? It was a very basic description of Wiccan principles and beliefs but within a few pages I felt as if I'd hit on something that matched what I'd always believed. The book led to the internet which led to the store, which led to an invitation to a class the following morning. The rest as they say is history.

    I quickly became a regular at the class and signed up to take a 101 the following February. Going to the store, joining the classes and signing up for the 101 showed the healing I'd gained thru college and SAFE. When I had started college I avoided people, didn't make eye contact, never went out and was injuring routinely and severely. Here I was seeking out people. It was however, a struggle. Crowds terrified me, people still terrified me. I was mostly staying safe but the urge was back stronger and lasting longer sometimes for days. When the urge hits it is a feeling as if my wrists, even my whole body is on fire. I knew I was sinking and without help I would end up back where I'd been before. I was seeking someone who understood and finding no one I felt incredibly frightened and alone. The Goddess was with me but had not yet revealed herself to me. I was becoming increasingly suicidal. Change was coming.

Chapter 6: Hecate Enters

The 101 started in February and in March I attended my first full moon ritual, hosted by the store and led by my teacher. If my life had been changing before it was nothing compared to what I was about to encounter. After this night I'd never be the same, for this night I would meet the dark Goddess herself and Hecate would become my Lady.

When the Goddess wishes to make a point or grab ones attention she has no trouble doing so and this night she choose to do so by possessing a person in the circle. I watched as this woman's facial structure, voice, tone, and manner of speech changed dramatically, her eyes even turned completely black. She spoke in detail to another in the circle and then called for another to come forward. No one did. I looked around the circle thinking to myself "what the fuck?! What kind of game is this?" Keeping in mind I was only about a month into my 101 and had not been to any rituals of any type, my shock and confusion were natural. As I looked around the circle that night, all I saw was shock written on the face of all present including the face of my teacher. When Hecate left the woman's body she was thrown backwards and was for a time completely out of it, ungrounded in her own body. Assistance was provided and she soon came around with no memory of what had happened. I felt strangely calm despite such a shocking experience and soon after circle went home, played with my ferrets and went to bed as normal. Normal however, had been left behind forever. I simply didn't know it yet.

The next day I awoke with a headache that sat in the middle of my forehead. Being prone to migraines I thought nothing of it, took some Excedrin and went on about my day. I gave second thought when the headache grew larger like ripples from a stone in a pond and was unresponsive to even a second dose of the Excedrin. Excedrin had never failed to stop a migraine for me before. By that evening I was in a full blow migraine vomiting, freezing cold, sensitive to light and sound - the whole nine yards. Finally in the early morning it stopped and I slept. From that time forward I've had some sensation at my third eye almost constantly. Sometimes the sensation is very mild and at other times it burns like fire. For about the first nine or ten months its pressure and sensation nearly drove me crazy. It was scary, not understanding what was happening or why. At times I wondered if I was ill, but how it opened and the lack of other signs or symptoms of being ill told me that was not the case. All attempts I made to control or ground the energy only made it stronger. For the first month I had no idea what was going on. I'd figured out that my third eye had opened but why, and for what eluded me. There is an old adage that says "when the student is ready the teacher appears." It's true. But, what they fail to mention is how appropriate and perfect the teacher provided will be, especially when the teacher is also a witch.

Witches are by their very nature teachers and healers and mine was no exception. I was sitting in class one day and began to rub at my third eye trying to ease the discomfort. My teacher looked at me and asked "Do you have a headache?" "No, my third eye has been bothering me since that ritual." He looked at me with this grin on his face and responded "You were the other one she was calling to that night." "Excuse me? I think we need to talk." What he told me essentially was that I have questions I need answered and she was trying to answer them. He was right of course. Coming to Wicca and the craft alone requires learning to see the world differently, that alone can generate questions. Add in the struggle I was having to stay safe and avoid falling into old patterns, the confusion I was feeling over o.k., now what , now that I'm out of school and home from SAFE, and only just starting to work, what do I do now, and it becomes clear the mass of inner turmoil that was working on me. What I'd really wanted to ask that night but didn't was "What do you do when there is no guide, no one who cares and understands." Now here I am almost a month later told she wanted to speak with me. I admit I was disappointed in having let the opportunity pass by. I was reassured however, that I could still go and speak with her. I was warned about the need for honesty in dealing with her, that the only offering she accepts is the truth of ones very heart.

The following Saturday night, while my Dad was out, I did speak to her. I told her of my fears and frustrations, and I told her that I didn't understand why she had wanted to talk to me but that I'd stay close to my teacher and learn. I told her I'd do anything she asked if she'd help me get thru. Now one needs to understand that a vow to a deity should NEVER be taken lightly. At that point however, I was desperate. I didn't want to fall back but I knew I was. The urges were coming more and more often and with increasing intensity. The power of the urge was a feeling as if my wrist or even my whole body was on fire sometimes to the point I would physically shake and they lasted sometimes for days. It would be awhile before I would see the answer she gave.

Thru the rest of that summer 101 continued and I enjoyed it as much as the depression and urges would allow. My sleep patterns were erratic to the point where I went a week with no sleep at all. I was looking for assistance but there seemed to be none. The 101 class concluded just before Samhain and classes at the store soon ended for the holidays. In a ritual designed for seeking what we need I again asked for help and heard, "I have sent you a teacher." It really is true that sometimes the best place to hide something is in plain sight. Just because we do not see or understand, does not mean we haven't been answered. In her statement of giving me a teacher was the beginning of the healing she would help me to find.

Chapter 7: Falling…But Light

After the holidays I began to go up to the weekly discussion group, it would be the breeding grounds for the start of my true healing. At one class, my teacher was sitting and discussing a person he knew with another person in the group. He used the fact that she self injures as a way to identify her. I found this infuriating. "We need to talk." I said to him after the discussion. I was furious because all too often people see the wounds and the behavior and NOT the person underneath. As we talked my own issues and struggles came out. He asked me "Do you need help?" "Yes, but I can't seem to find anyone who deals with this who really understands." When all was said and done he said that he would see what he could do. I didn't expect him to find anyone. I had already spoken to the heads of Hopkins and Shepherd Pratt and had been to about nine different counselors. The light of hope was fading. I sure didn't expect what he would do, and I was too new to understand the impact of Hecate's hand at work.

The following week he pulled me aside and agreed to work with me, his only rule was complete honesty. I agreed. I don't like to think about what would have happened to me if he had not agreed to help. I truly believe I'd be dead or living in a zombie state of mere existence where nothing matters, where joy and hope don't exist.

Adding to the mix, the previous fall my Father had discovered my books and altar in my room and without a question to me, told me he wanted them gone. I told him no. He promptly began throwing out "facts" as if he had a clue, all of which I countered with correct information. Finally I realized that the conversation was going nowhere and that he was not going to be open to it. I told him, "I think I'm old enough to choose for myself". I was, after all, in my mid-twenties. He responded to me by suggesting that perhaps I should practice elsewhere. On top of everything else I now found myself looking for a place to live with no savings, having used all I'd had just a few months before to help myself go to SAFE, and just having started working, but my position was only that of a temp. It would be a couple of years before my Father and I would once again speak.

My first living arrangement after I left my father was into the basement of a woman that I knew vaguely thru a wildlife rehabilitation group I'd been working with. The place was a disaster; 23 breeding pairs of birds, 7 kittens, and 2 semi-feral cats would share the space with me and my 2 ferrets and guinea pig. The arrangement was that I would help to care for the animals. The woman meant well but between the animals downstairs and the ones upstairs which included several dogs among others she couldn't keep up. The first time I went to shower I found the bathtub black from the feces of the kittens. The woman worked evenings and her one dog was a barker and cage banger so sleep for me was often impossible. When the outside wooden door came off and I was left with just a screen door I was told she wouldn't be able to fix it owing to the need to fix the roof. This was not what I wanted to hear when it was January with snow on the ground. The dog however, was the final straw. I told her that she needed to find a way to keep the dog quiet so that I could sleep and her response was that she couldn't do anything about it not being home. My reply was, "That's what trainers are for." I knew it would be the end of my welcome and three days later I received a letter essentially telling me to get out. I was lucky in that another friend had offered to let me stay with her for awhile. The day for me to move came and one person that helped me commented that "You'd have to pay me to live here."

All of this was going on at the same time. There was so much confusion and pain, fear, loneliness and depression. I was still injuring at times and yet hating myself for it. With more friends, help and support than ever I still felt desperate and alone. I truly was a pathetic and lonely creature, in some ways I barely felt human. Hecate came thru for me, and my teacher also was good to his word to help. A lot of my recovery hinges on the actions of my teacher but it is Hecates' role that I choose to share here. I will take a moment or two to say that he was a part of her plan and that for his part he asked for honesty and gave it. He spent hours talking with me, letting me vent and giving perspective, sometimes coming down hard and sometimes sharing enough of his own story to remind me I'm not alone. As time went on we would realize how parallel our lives had been in many respects and that too was part of Hecate's plan for the both of us I believe. You see, the Lady will not pass up an opportunity to make things into a two way street. The truth is life is a two way street and no interaction between people is ever one sided. Everyone will always walk away with something. It was an important part of my healing for her to have sent me a teacher that could honestly look at me and say I understand. The understanding and acceptance I found was probably his greatest gift in helping me to heal. He was an instrument of healing for me, but the surgery of healing was and is being carried out by Hecate herself. She places people, animals, resources and scenarios in front of me to help me. It is my choice then to heal but she's always there in subtle or not so subtle ways to encourage, correct, guide and teach. Let us take a look at this powerful and often misunderstood Goddess before exploring her powers as a healer in depth.

Chapter 8: Introducing Hecate

There are many good books and websites on Hecate and her history, some of which I will provide in the bibliography, so I will not go into great detail but provide only enough to enable the reader to get a working understanding of her. Some of the material I will present can readily be found by looking in any book or on any site about her, but some of it will be different and based on my experience and interpretations thereof.

Hecate is well known as being of the Greek pantheon but in truth she predates the Greeks hailing instead from Thrace and considered to possibly have evolved from the Egyptian Hekat, Goddess of midwifery. Hecate herself is considered a Goddess of crossroads, midwifes, wild animals, witches and magic. She was respected by Zeus and retains powers in all three realms. She is a guardian of the crossroads and the underworld. She is a Goddess of choices and transitions. She carries two torches to illuminate the way and help a traveler to see the crossroad they are at and the choices they have available to them clearly. She carries keys to knowledge and to the underworld. She carries a dagger to cut the silver cord of life when our time here is done. She is considered to be a triple Goddess, maiden, mother, and crone, showing the face needed at the time. In her triplicity she represents and has knowledge of the phases of life. She walks with black hounds and the hound of Hades, Cerberus himself is considered to belong to her. She herself sometimes appears with three heads representing past, present, and future as well as the three stages of life. As a Goddess of the crossroads she is also a Goddess who is all about facing fears. For choices and change always involve some element of fear. Will you take the well worn path or will you choose another more challenging one? From my experiences working with her I knew that a favorite question to ask of those she works with is "Who are you." She is not interested in your job or your bank account but instead who are you in the depths of your being all other things stripped away. This question is the basis of the quest she likes to send those she works with on. It is the quest that is the path for the healing she can provide.

Before she began pushing me she had to accomplish two things; 1. Get my attention and introduce herself, and 2. She had to get me to trust her. The first she accomplished by the opening of my third eye after possessing a participant in my first circle. The discomfort and intensity made it impossible for me to deny or turn away. The second part was harder and even now sometimes I struggle with it. For after all I've been thru I'd be a fool to trust anyone easily. For the first several months of meditations that I did nearly daily she would appear and simply stand or sit with me. At these times she offered little more than quiet companionship and acceptance. Her only instruction to me during this time was for me to stay close to my teacher. This I had no issue with as I was enjoying the 101 and the acceptance I found there. It seems like a minor thing but to one who lives in a world where abuse and pain is around every corner and who is used to being criticized and put down at every thought, opinion, or action, quiet acceptance was more precious than gold.

How many of us take the time to just sit with those we know are hurting, without judging, counseling, or trying to do something? The healing magic and powers of acceptance and quiet are too often overlooked. At the same time the presence of my teacher which was also clearly her doing, began to be of greater importance. He was able to provide the reassurance I needed in dealing with the opening of my third eye by letting me know it was something he too had been thru with her.

Hecate took the time and in so doing I found a comfort in her presence that I've never felt with anyone or anything else. In doing so she confronted and put to rest any stereotypes or preconceived notion I had about her as evil, or vindictive or any of a host of other things that popular culture likes to say about her.

Chapter 9: At the Crossroads

Hecate had done much prep work on me and with me to this point, but if I thought the ride would be easy I was wrong. I would have to arrive at the crossroads and choose. In order to do so I would have to face the guardian of the gate that was my own fear. No one could do this for me. I had to decide alone because the work would be extremely hard and painful and I had to be willing. It was the encounter with my father which brought me to the crossroad of choice and Hecate stood quietly by and awaited my decision.

As I look back at that night where he confronted me about my altar, my books, and told me to practice elsewhere, I'm able to see the crossroads I had stood at clearly. That night I had a choice; listen to my father and remove all the books and give up something I'd found pleasure in, or move out and live my own life.

Even more fundamental a decision than that, was whether or not I was truly ready to embrace life, to truly go thru what would be needed to build the life I wanted. A life of respect and hope and joy that I could control for better or worse or was I content to live by the rules of others. Did I have what it took to truly walk with Hecate as a witch? Was I prepared to pay the price? Could I conquer my fear of the unknown, which was the guardian of this gate I was standing at and in time come to live?

Looking back I see that it was a profound moment of choice for me, but the answer I gave my Father, "I believe I'm old enough to choose for myself." Came out of me without a conscious thought on my part, and I never gave any thought or made any effort to change that decision even when I realized he wanted me to move out. I knew I had no money, having spent it going to SAFE; my job was temporary with no guarantee of being taken on permanent. I had no place to go. I was terrified and more than a little distraught, but I knew I had to live my life for me. I knew that if I could not live life true to myself, my desires, my hopes, dreams and beliefs that it wouldn't be worth living. I'd never feel any better or attain anything and that eventually it would send me back on the course of self injury I was fighting so hard to overcome.

As I walked the path with Hecate I would find myself back at the crossroads many times. Often times I would not recognize I was there until I'd already made the choice, other times I did. In some cases Hecate herself made it clear that I was there and needed to choose and that once I did I'd never be able to go back. Each time the scenario challenged me, made me look inward on myself, made me consider how badly I really want this. Each time I choose to follow the path forward I have never regretted it. Going forward sometimes brought hurt and pain in the short term, but long term has brought only positive growth and change to my mind, spirit and even my mundane life.

Chapter 10: The Seeds of Doubt

From the woman's basement to my friend's spare room, the tide was about to turn and my healing would pick up speed. I was deeply depressed and finally my friend sat me down and spoke to me. I don't remember her words but the effect was to bring me back just enough from the depths and get me moving. I would live with her for nine months. I spent the time to build up some savings for my own place and working on healing the issues of my past.

During this time my sister told me about some letters my Grandmother had written my Mother in the attic at my Dad's house. I decided to go and check them out for any clues to the parts of my past and childhood I could not remember. My teacher had been planting many seeds of doubt in my mind, challenging the notions of inferiority my parents had instilled in me. He had even told me that the energy I gave off was that of sexual abuse or something similar. It was interesting to me since my sister had always said she thought she'd been raped but couldn't remember by whom. What I found in the attic among the letters was my baby book which I'd never seen. I'd always been told by my parents that I was very sickly as a baby and child. My Father told me that the doctors had said they should put me in an institution that I'd never walk, talk etc…But here I found my baby book and according to it I did everything right on schedule. I decided to go to the hospital where I was born and check my birth records. These records did not match with what I'd been told. There was no sign of a seriously ill child in those records. My APGAR was 4. I had some mild respiratory distress the first 24 hours which resolved easily and some jaundice which also was easily resolved. They kept me 15 days which was how much of a preemie I was and then sent me home. To find records that contradicted all I'd been told tore at me greatly. It was as if I lost a portion of my identity. It was painful having what little trust I'd had in my family tore up further. Yet in this destruction lay the basis of a rebirth. I was able to then begin bit by bit to question and challenge long held assumptions and beliefs. Many journeys Hecate sat and stood with me offering reassurance. Her quiet strength and presence were the calm point amidst the storm of turmoil and pain I was experiencing. What exactly happened with my health after those first records I may never know for sure but Hecate has over time showed me glimpses of my past that further suggest I was not sickly of my own accord. The truth of any of these things can never be proven and in some ways may not be important. What mattered was the doubt about the stories I was told, that allowed me to question their opinion about me and more importantly my opinion of myself.

My teacher continued to spend many hours, sometimes whole nights talking to me, letting me vent and or cry, sometimes yelling and sometimes sharing a glimpse of his own story with me. In so doing he forged bonds of trust that would allow me to take the needed leaps of faith to do the exercises he gave me, to dare to reach out and to keep going when every cell of my being screamed NO, STOP!

In a series of journeys Hecate was trying to bring my Mother thru to speak with me. Each time that she did I would return to myself, refusing to speak with her. Eventually my teacher gave me an exercise to do telling me to call Hecate and my Mother and to let her come thru. I followed his instructions and allowed her to come. The whole time Hecate stood beside me, letting me know by her presence that I was not alone and was safe. The visions I saw in that journey were brutal. I saw myself lying on my bed as a child with my mother lying on top of me screaming and hitting the bed beside me. "Your father likes his women young." I heard and I thought, "But you're Mommy?" How can a young child be responsible for treatment like this? Again, I began to question. The questioning led me to begin to realize that it wasn't my fault.

There had never really been anything wrong with me, my family however is messed up. As I began to realize this my behavior slowly began to change.

Chapter 11: Changing Identities

A major part in the healing of anything but especially of the mind and personality is the taking on of a new and improved identity. It is unrealistic to expect to improve and feel better if one's internal way of viewing one's self never changes or if the internal self talk never changes. An outside person can tell you how smart, competent, or skilled you are forever, but until one starts to change on the inside the messages will never get thru.

Finding the letters in my fathers attic, and then viewing my birth records had started the process by planting doubt in the validity of what my parents and family had told me all along. But only doubt was planted. At that point I could have truly gone either way. Other things needed to happen to back up the change, and other things did happen.

The same summer I was going thru the process of the letters and dealing with the beginnings of doubt, I also received my Reiki one attunement. Within a day or two of this attunement, I had an experience that made me question the nature of life, reality, energy even existence in general. This managed to further add fuel to the fire that was already lit, causing me to begin to re-evaluate myself, my life, my beliefs and my manner of functioning.

I was at work and looking for a friend to speak with as I'd not had a chance to see her all morning. As I was looking for her she returned from lunch with a full blown asthma attack. Without any medications she was discussing with her co-worker what to do. As I was watching this, I heard a voice tell me "Go on you can help this now. " Finally I asked her if I could try some Reiki and see what would happen. In just a couple of minutes, if that, she reported the pain had stopped and her breathing was visibly easier. I continued the Reiki for about 5 minutes and her breathing was back to normal with no relapse. Both she and I were shocked, and as I walked away to return to my work I couldn't help but look down at my hands and wonder about a great many things. How did that happen? What exactly is this? What does it mean to have the ability to have done that? How powerful are we really to be able to harness that type of energy for healing? These and at least a thousand other thoughts ran thru my mind in the coming minutes, hours, even days after that, and again more seeds were planted.

    I began going to a Reiki clinic with some friends soon after and in the process of working there I got the experience of seeing and also experiencing the healing power of Reiki on myself as well as others .Working as a practitioner also placed me in a position of being seen as a healer to others and also forced me to begin to see myself in that light. It forced me to begin looking at myself in a new way. As with anything, practice and repetition bring a degree of comfort. As I continued to attend this clinic and practice there, I became more comfortable with the people and with working on people and most important I became more comfortable with this new identity that I was taking on. The combination of the experience with the Reiki, along with the constant sensation and continuing discomfort of my third eye, which I could not deny caused me to slowly, bit by bit, change my own view of myself.

    Thru my journey many other scenarios would happen to further this change in identity some of which I will discuss in chapters to come, but these were the biggies that set the stage and began my movement forward.

Chapter 12: Other Divine Assistance

Hecate is a very powerful Goddess in her own right, but there are times when other deities are better equipped to teach us a lesson that we need to learn. I have at times with Hecates' instruction and encouragement worked with, been worked on, or been taught by a number of other deities along the way. The first of these was Kwan Yin.

Kwan Yin, while not strictly speaking a Goddess, is never the less a powerful being in her own right. She is considered a Bodhisattva from the Buddhist tradition. An enlightened being that has put off entering nirvana until all humans are ready to enter.

From the Lady Kwan Yin I learned lessons of compassion and love. "True compassion can be brutal, and true love can be as well and sometimes should be." were the words she would speak to me over time. Both of these lessons took a bit of thought and contemplation on my part. It is against what society teaches to consider compassion to be something "brutal".

The word brutal is being used as in harsh and painful. I was always raised and taught to believe that compassion was gentle. The hug amidst the tears, the reassuring touch of a friends' hand, that was what I thought compassion was. Love too I always thought was gentle, and forgiving. Yet here I was being told otherwise. Consider for a moment the definition of compassion. A web search brought up several. Let us consider them for just a moment.

Definitions of compassion on the Web:

- A deep awareness of and sympathy for another's suffering
- The humane quality of understanding the suffering of others and wanting to do something about it
- Compassion is a sense of shared suffering, most often combined with a desire to alleviate or reduce such suffering.
- Transcends both natural human sympathy and normal Christian concern, enabling one to sense in others a wide range of emotions and then provide a supportive ministry of caring and intercessory prayer. Also called the gift of mercy.
- The wish to free others from their suffering.
- The unconditional wish that all sentient beings be freed from physical and mental suffering.
- [from Latin com with + pati to bear, suffer] Sympathetic understanding; the feeling of one's unity with all that is, resulting in an "intimate magnetic sympathy with all that is."
- A Primary Law and prime virtue, is when a person is moved by the suffering or distress of another, and by the desire to relieve it. Compassion is empathy not sympathy-identification with and understanding of another's situation, feelings, and motives. Compassion is the highest vibration of the elastic relative Law of Tolerance, under the Principle of Equilibrium. "Blessed are the merciful, for they shall obtain mercy" is the Law of Compassion.
- The desire to help when a need is discovered.

There are other definitions but they all speak about the desire to assist with a known need of another and the desire to relieve suffering. What about the definition of love?

Definitions of love on the Web:

- a strong positive emotion of regard and affection; "his love for his work"; "children need a lot of love"
- any object of warm affection or devotion; "the theater was her first love"
- have a great affection or liking for; " I love French food"; " She loves her boss and works hard for him"
- beloved: a beloved person; used as terms of endearment
- a deep feeling of sexual desire and attraction; "their love left them indifferent to their surroundings"; "she was his first love"
- get pleasure from; " I love cooking"
- a score of zero in tennis or squash; "it was 40 love"
- be enamored or in love with; "She loves her husband deeply"
- Roll in the hay: have sexual intercourse with; "This student sleeps with everyone in her dorm"; "Adam knew Eve"; "were you ever intimate with this man?"
- Sexual love: sexual activities (often including sexual intercourse) between two people; "his lovemaking disgusted her"; "he hadn't had any love in months"; "he has a very complicated love life"

It seems clear from these definitions that love is all about strong positive emotions of warmth, devotion and affection. As I began to think about scenarios from my own life, my path thus far, and in the news, I realized, much to my surprise…she's right! The mother who scolds her child for reaching for the Aspirin bottle on the counter, and admonishes the child to leave it be and NO is being both compassionate and loving to her child. She has strong positive feelings for the child and desires to keep the child from suffering. She knows the harm the medication can cause, and cares enough to protect her child even though in the moment the child may suffer some hurt feelings or the sting of the mother's hand upon their backside. Thus by the definitions we see above the mother showed both love and compassion for her child even though the child would most likely say something along the lines of "you hurt my feelings.". The child is of course right, in the short term the mother did indeed hurt the child's feelings, but she also protected the child from harm. Therefore, by this example we can see that sometimes compassion must indeed be brutal and love sometimes must indeed hurt.

What does any of this have to do with Hecate and my walk with her towards healing? Well, there have been many scenarios that she has put me thru that have been painful, brutal, saddening etc…but which were in truth needed for me to truly heal. They normally showed themselves as encounters with other people, but they usually led me back to her with cries of "what the hell, why did this happen, this hurts, please I can't handle this. " Often times her answer was silence. The lessons on compassion allowed me to see that she was not in truth being simply hurtful, that there was indeed a reason for the pain. I've been in circles where she was called and questioned and even challenged about situations that had unfolded and her basic answer was it was needed and you need to consider what you **do** have, what you **have** been given. Without the lessons from Kwan Yin I would not have been able to take the several steps back needed and realize the truth of the larger scenario presented. I learned to see the truth of the love in the spanking of the mother.

Kwan Yin has not been the only other deity Hecate has introduced me to. Durga, Isis, Ra, Hermes, Odin, Cerridwen, Athena, and others have also made appearances. Each teaching a lesson, doing some energy work, or sometimes providing a needed tool for a scenario I was about to undergo. Hecate was nearly always present when the others came, her presence letting me know all was well and that whatever the others were saying and doing was part of her plan for me.

By bringing the others to me at times she also managed in a very subtle way to instill a measure of flexibility in me. I developed a willingness not only to trust her, but also to trust others. At first she was always present and I would not accept any other without her o.k. As I worked with some of the others more, she began to not come as quickly or at all. It mirrored the mundane aspect of my healing, for at first I only worked closely with my teacher keeping distant and silent to others. Slowly over time that began to change as he began to encourage me to work with others and as living arrangements changed, I had to begin to deal with others more and more. For each step Hecate took with me when I would journey and work with her on the astral, she made sure that I encountered similar scenarios on the mundane, so the work always occurred on two fronts.

Chapter 13: Beginning to Move on

Each major step up in the level of healing and work, each improvement in functioning, has been preceded by a Reiki attunement. Each attunement functioning to first remove the accumulated debris of the past work both mentally and physically and also to provide me another level of energy to draw on for support and growth. The major changes to this point on the path had been preceded by my Reiki one attunement given to me by another instructor as part of an ongoing class of general topics and not having been something I sought out on my own. At that point in time I was too afraid of people, too withdrawn to have asked for it on my own, but it was needed and Hecate made sure circumstances allowed me to receive it.

Reiki two however was a different story. I journeyed one evening and in the midst of my Lady speaking and working with me she said to me "You have the heart of a healer if you would only allow." She instructed me to seek the second attunement at that time. I approached my teacher, relayed the journey and asked for the second attunement. He questioned me as to why I wanted it, what I had learned. My response to him was that it was time and I could no longer deny who I was. I've never seen anyone so ecstatic.

The day for the attunement came and I met up with him. He warned me that it would be an emotional healing and said that he did indeed plan to pass the attunement but he needed to make sure I realized. We talked until he was sure I understood, until I finally told him that I understood the challenge, that I could go no further without it and that it would help to prep me for the future. The look on his face, the tears in his eyes and the catch in his voice spoke to me of both true worry and concern and yet also made me uncomfortable as well. I wondered why after everything to that point he would doubt my ability to overcome now.

I honestly can not speak of the emotional cleansing that took place as I can not see it even looking back; perhaps I was simply too close to register. However it must have happened as I became less and less likely to sit quiet when something needed said or done even among a crowd. A situation arose with the friend I was living with that shook our relationship and we decided it was a sign for me to begin looking for a place of my own. I found an apartment knowing it was the right one when the model I viewed turned out to be the actual apartment for rent. Sometimes the Goddess yells, sometimes she whispers. I moved in, in February. I had no furniture, not even a bed. For the first six months or so I slept on blankets on the floor until a couple of friends gave me a mattress. I was living on savings and looking for a better paying job. I could not afford furniture. Once again Hecate would prove to me that she is indeed looking out for me.

I was out hiking at Gunpowder State Park one summer afternoon when I heard the hooting of a Great Horned Owl. Now Great Horns are native to the area but as it was the middle of the afternoon it struck me as an odd time for one to be calling. The owl is one animal associated with Hecate so its call at such an odd time got my attention. "Mother, what are you trying to tell me?" Within a half hour's time I'd have my answer.

Standing in the middle of Blockbuster Video, my cell phone rang. My brother's girlfriend called to introduce herself. Soon after the call she decided to move into my brother's place and much of her furniture would become mine. My apartment was furnished almost entirely from my friends and my brother's girlfriend, which included a queen size bed my brother decided to give up from the spare room when she moved in. A queen size bed is something I'd never have been able to afford on my own.

Eventually there came a time as comes in everyone's healing where there is nothing more anyone else can do to help them, they must simply choose. Just before Ostara, I came to realize, that there was nothing anyone up to and including Hecate herself could do for me. I simply was at that point where I had to choose for myself if I was going to heal and move forward into the life that Hecate was guiding me towards and showing me was possible, or to fall back and return to the self injury. Once again I stood at the crossroads with Hecate holding her torches high awaiting my decision.

The group of friends I hung out with was planning an Ostara ritual at a local park. A couple of nights before the ritual, I spoke with my teacher and told him of my realization. He asked me what my choice would be. I told him to go forward. We agreed that as a way of doing this that I would gather up all the razors I had together and bring them to the ritual. I would take one and bury it in the woods and he would take the rest and dispose of them. That day turned out to be very rainy and chilly. As I walked thru the rain into the wood to bury the razor, the emotions inside me were as tossed as the weather. I wanted to go forward but yet the razor HAD served me well in many ways for a long time. I found a tree that reminded me of the whomping willow of Harry Potter fame. I reached out to it and asked if it would ground these energies for me. I began to feel warm and a smile appeared on my face as the tree supplied its answer. I buried the razor among the roots of the tree and returned to the gathering without looking back. I promptly turned over the rest of the blades to my teacher and then moved to the fire to dry. Driving home that evening I felt lost and unsure of where to go from there, but of course my Lady knew full well what was to come.

This would not be the end of my injuring. There would be a few more instances where my limits would be pushed and I would relapse, but they became fewer and fewer. It was however an important mile marker of a shift within my psyche. I once had a psychology teacher say that recovery is not a straight line, sometimes you take steps forward and sometimes back and gradually the time between back slides gets greater. She was right. I have found along my journey toward healing and in working with Hecate that each step or leap forward was always preceded by a lesson in the facing of fear that normally led me to fall back and crash first. It's similar to the magical rule of that which one wishes to banish must first be invoked. One must meet the guardian of the gate before he can be defeated and entrance to the realms he guards gained. I've learned to watch for the times that I have fallen in to old ways and recognize them as signpost of a new level of healing and work coming. In so doing I've learned not to beat myself up for the falls no matter how badly they have hurt but to more quickly pick myself up and look to the road ahead for the new adventure it would bring.

> Hecate, great Lady of transformation,
>
> change and deep healing,
>
> Join me this night and assist me to
>
> cleanse the blocks that hold me back,
>
> as I seek to move forward and embrace
>
> myself. Assist me. Guide me.
>
> Hail and Welcome!

Chapter 14: Who Am I?

After that first Ostara I began to relax and socialize more and more with other people. The larger group of people, who had played a role in helping me learn to be with people, fell apart soon after that ritual, but a smaller group remained. Eventually as I healed and time moved on my relationship likewise improved and I found myself relating to the similarities of other people's struggles to those of my own, especially to my teacher. As time had gone on, we both realized more and more how similar our struggles had been. It was as if we walked parallel lives and a friendship grew. This too was part of Hecate's plan not just for me but for him as well. It was also to prove to be training for the future. There are no encounters in life that are one sided, both parties always come away with something though sometimes one may need to step back and even set aside ones emotions to see it.

As I interacted more with my teacher and others I began to slowly see and understand my abilities that had been a source of strained and lost relationships throughout my life. I have a knack it turns out for seeing to the core of people to see what they are hiding, or running from and speaking to it. I did so routinely and without realizing it. The conversations with my teacher clearly showed this and his response was often to get upset even angry at times to the point of not wishing to speak with me. Such a reaction for awhile upset me greatly. No one likes the idea of losing someone they care for. Yet, here again I was being placed in a scenario to let me heal and to learn about myself. I learned by watching his reactions over time and also by having it pointed out by another friend that after the blow up he'd change. I learned that what I'm seeing and saying IS correct and thus I was learning to begin trusting in myself. It's the first time I remember ever doing that. Trusting in ones self is a vital ability to have. It is the foundation for being able to handle the ups and downs of life without resorting to maladaptive strategies of which self injury is one.

Throughout it all, I frequently journeyed to Hecate, sometimes seeking and finding quiet reassurances as time spent sitting under a tree or on the beach. Often times she would do work on my chakras removing things out and placing things in. Often we would do work together to help me. As I began to truly shift focus we did a series of journeys over several months that helped me begin to change my identity.

I was taken to the rune Dagaz, sitting in the middle of a field and instructed to pass thru it. Dagaz is a fire rune and is a very powerful rune for change and transformation. Its literal meaning is day and the catchwords that come up for its divinatory meaning are day, daylight, change, growth and it also signifies work for no true change can occur without work and effort. I would pass thru the rune with Hecate at my side and we would stop and look back. I would see myself. At first I was cowering in a corner, cut up, crying, hurting, alone, and afraid. I would be instructed or questioned about showing compassion and letting go. My response each time would be to hug this vision of my former self, give her Reiki, and hold her. As this series of journeys progressed, this vision of my former self changed becoming more and more skeletal until such a time as I came thru and saw only a grave. It was a series of journeys that showed a gradual shifting of my internal view of myself, however, one can not give up ones old personality and ways of viewing themselves without having something to replace it with. To do so would create a vacuum of identity that could lead to a fall back to the known and familiar or even worse version thereof as nature abhors a vacuum. The encounters with my teacher and with others began to show me that I am the one who sees to the depths of ones very being, the truth of their desires and fears and that knowledge was the cornerstone of my rebuilding. It was also the cornerstone along with Kwan Yin's lessons on compassion that allows me to speak truth to someone even when I know they may well not like what I'm about to say. In this manner I learned to be able to be true to myself and my role without falling apart under their reactions. The full implications of this ability would not come clear for awhile longer yet.

Hecate taking me to the edge of my endurance and pushing me a bit further thru the scenarios I encountered was actually a vital part of my moving on. This helped me to learn to keep the big picture in mind and take three steps back and see the big picture as the role of Keybearer that she would help me realize I possess.

None of this was easy and many times I thought of giving up, of isolating again, and going back to self injury. At these times Hecate would simply look at me and ask "Would you throw it all away?" With the wisdom of the crone she understands that I need to freely choose my path. I needed to be willing to do the work or nothing anyone would say or do would have an effect. I always made the choice to keep going, finding some relief in simply having my frustration acknowledged, by simply being given a choice. Each time she prepared to take me to a new level she would present me a doorway of some sort and give me the choice to pass thru or decline. Always with the admonishment to consider carefully, choose wisely because, once done I could not go back. Over time I was dubbed the group's guard dog and keeper of the schedule for my propensity to speak up to things that concerned me and for my knack of keeping people, dates and locations straight in my head with little effort. The roles too gave me something more to grab onto as a manner of forming a new identity. All this took much determination, work (mundane and magical both), courage and many, many tears. Every time I thought I was getting it I would seem to crash as Hecate took me to a new level and drove the healing deeper.

Chapter 15: Mundane Influence

Even in my mundane world, things were happening that allowed and supported my healing. Each of my mundane jobs themselves presented me with people and situations that challenged me to stay focused, grow, and learn.

At my first job, I found myself very quickly doing the work of two people as my coworker was let go, and training a series of temps and finally my own replacement as well. This required much focus to keep things running up to the level required and to ensure the safety of all involved. I won't say it was always easy. I went thru the week of no sleep and the scenario of my father asking me to "practice elsewhere" while I was at this job. At times my emotions did get the better of me. But my boss and coworkers were supportive as I worked it all thru and I for my part worked hard to be sure that despite it all I made sure the work was done at the end of the day.

My second job found me needing to confront my fears of being around and performing in front of others. I also once again found myself having to help coordinate the work and help to oversee that the work asked of others was done. It was intense because I was still carrying a fear of others, and a lack of belief in my own self, but it was needed. Each of these two jobs lasted until the issues they were designed to help me master had indeed been mastered and then with the use of financial issues I would find myself forced to look for another. I could not have mastered the second without the basis gained in the first and the second set me up for the third and current job. I find myself now in a position of having to help others with no experience in my work, learn a bit about it, to help set up a new program and of having to be prepared to oversee others as the program grows.

I had not believed in the changes in my self confidence gained from the last job until I came to this one and found myself not only performing in front of others the techniques needed but also helping others to learn. My hands were not shaking my thoughts were not jumbled, it was as if I'd done these things for a million lifetimes. This job is presenting me with new issues to face and conquer. The issue now of communicating with people without offending, I'm finding challenging. It is one I've been trying to work on for awhile and have been struggling with. As usual the people in place are ones able to help. Each of my bosses has encouraged me, and each has spoken to me of seeing a lot of good and basically taken the time to quietly support me as I've struggled to learn the lessons I've needed. My current boss is proving to be no exception to that rule. As I have each time before the challenges and lessons this new job presents will be learned, met and overcome and I'm looking forward to the journey they present.

Chapter 16: Now to the Present

"You are now the Keybearer." Hecate spoke as she placed a key around my neck. The implications of this I'm only now beginning to see and understand. My healing continued as did the taking of a new identity the speed and power of this increased with the passing of my Uncle.

My Uncle had been sick with lung cancer for awhile and my family and I knew his death was approaching. I had journeyed to Hecate with questions on an entirely unrelated topic but was instructed instead on issues relating to my Uncles passing. I was told to do some chakra clearing work and that I should then pull up the blue flame and to form a spiral of it. My response was o.k., not yet grasping what she had said to me. I soon realized that she was instructing me to open a portal in the veil and help him to cross. The next evening I got the call to come to the hospital. They didn't expect him to make it thru the night. He did indeed make it thru the night and the following afternoon we arranged home hospice care. He was adamant that he wanted to go home and not die in the hospital. He arrived home that afternoon and the vigil of me, my sister, and my nephew continued at his bedside. In the early morning hours after having been awake for nearly three days I found myself working on three levels in a way I'd never done before and never imagined doing. The first level of the mundane was simply talking to him, to my sister and my nephew to assist in care and to calm my sister so that her own naturally strong emotions did not serve to hold him here. The second level was the level of Reiki in an attempt to calm him and help the extreme amount of pain he was in. Even with morphine being given at frequent intervals the pain he was in was excruciating. The third level was the pulling up of the blue flame and the opening of the portal across the veil which I was able to literally see in the doorway between rooms. As he passed I felt his spirit pass thru me. After he passed I let my sister know he was gone and she called into hospice. As the nurse arrived and confirmed the death and began to tend to his body I went outside and sat down exhausted and overwhelmed with the work I'd just done. Any denial of my true self and doubt as to my abilities or to the properness of my working with Hecate dissolved in that time. The change of identity became firmly established but the identity was not yet complete nor the changes that it foreshadowed.

That spring enough changes had taken place that I felt it was time to do a ritual for moving on. The original pentacle I'd been wearing no longer felt right and so I had found a new one to take on, a pentacle with a snake intertwined around it and an amethyst in the center. I called to Hecate, I called to the dragons and I declared my intent to move on. In the journey that followed my declaration, the dragons, and Hecate worked on my chakras intently. The next day and in the coming days it felt as if I were undergoing a Reiki cleansing. My energies were going crazy. I was waking up drenched in sweat and gasping for air I was so hot. Salt baths were the only thing that seemed to help. After a few days Hecate helped me to understand that I was undergoing a kundalini awakening. The effects that I would deal with after that would teach me much and yet make it harder for me to relate even to my teacher as he has not undergone such a thing and thus could not understand. At first the energy simply made me feel hot, and then I went thru a phase of extreme irritability. Hecate appeared in one journey and told me "I am taking your voice you must learn to speak differently." Within 24 hours I was completely unable to speak. I would be without my voice almost entirely for over two months. One journey stimulated the kundalini issues to the point where I came back unable to move. The energy was running up and down my legs and going as far as the second chakra and I could feel it. I simply could not move anything. It took me about an hour to regain my arms and then several hours to be able to walk. The weekend passed before my ability to walk was reliable and then I had some on and off issues with my hands until a friend suggested doing some chakra cleansing work to clear the pathway for the energy. That resolved the issue but even today if I do not keep up on that exercise I begin to have trouble with my hands and legs.

Being without my voice was the harder part to deal with, you do not realize how much you rely on it until you can no longer speak. I couldn't even whisper and my only means to communicate was to write things down. It was frightening not knowing how long this would go on. If something happened I could not get help as easily since I could not communicate by phone. I got to experience firsthand how little consideration people tend to give each other. I learned that people have a preconceived notion of how much time they are willing to give you, all of about three seconds it seemed. Because I could not speak my attempts to communicate took longer and people would often have the attitude that I was a bother. It was a very eye opening experience for me. I learned too that even those close usually would not bother to take the time to allow you to compensate. For even friends sometimes would blow off my attempts to communicate. I had no idea what she meant about learning to speak differently and knowing that I would not get my voice back until I figured it out frustrated me. Finally I realized that she was referring to my internal self talk. She was asking me to gain control over my internal chatter, all the internal talk of how useless I was, screwed up, not good enough etc…she was asking me to change. She was also asking me to learn to control my emotions more. To see that all would work out and didn't require the depths of fear I'd usually shown. Since I couldn't speak there was often nothing I could do to change things or effect things at all and so all I could do was let them play out. By the loss of my voice she taught me to trust myself, to be more understanding of others handicaps and to trust her on a whole new level as well.

Samhain rolled around again and my friends and I were doing some ghost hunting. My teacher and I came upon a locked door that we wished to open but we had no key. I jokingly cried out "Hey Hecate we could really use a key down here could you send us one" A moment later my teacher looks over and said there's our key. He walks over picks up a piece of wood, dusts off the tip and promptly and with no trouble unlocks the door. We looked at each other in amazement and I called out "Thank you Mother." Later I addressed Hecate again with my thanks for the key and she replied "You are now the Keybearer you can call for these things now you know." Let it never be said that the Goddess doesn't have a sense of humor! Still the idea of Keybearer did not sink in. My office moved into a new building at my new job but I had not been granted pass access to the building which I realized one cold January morning while I stood outside with no one around. Again I called out "You know Hecate I could really use a key to unlock this door it's entirely too cold even by my standards to be standing outside for who knows how long until someone shows up. " Less than a minute later my boss came down the stairs and saw me and let me in. "Thank you Mother." Hmmmm one would think that I would get the point but no, call me dense but I just didn't pay enough attention. Well when the whisper doesn't work and the clue by four fails out comes the frying pan. Trouble amongst the group of friends soon would see the group broke apart and yet another scenario would leave my teacher wishing nothing to do with me. Yet again Hecate is working. Before the last get together I had journeyed and she had met with me. We had a very long talk about a lot of things, including the idea of being Keybearer. I have reached the point in my journey where I have shed off enough of the crap that I no longer need the same supports that I've needed to this point and in fact it is coming time for me to begin to pay it forward. In the journey she asked me to do something for her…begin to dream. I had not been dreaming for a very long time. I'd stopped when the depression overtook years ago. She asked me "what is it you want?" I thought for a moment and then answered her. "I wish for my spirit to soar like a bird on the wing….I wish to look at another that is where I've been and say to them that while I can not take the blade from them I can guide them until it becomes merely a signpost along the way." She said to me that I had called for keys to open doors on the mundane twice and that was o.k., for I needed to understand that it is real but that I must look deeper.

What I have discovered is that I do indeed see deeper into people to their truths and fears and in so doing by words and actions I force them to deal. I've realized I have the power to facilitate great healing for myself and for others and that what I've done to this point with no realization and thus managed to cause harm in doing, I must now learn to control and do it in such a way as people are able to handle. It is a great challenge as I am not one to tend to run very long from things and I have a hard time letting others take a slower pace. Patience was never my strong suit. It is however the newest challenge she has presented me and I will work at it until this too is mastered. The communication issues at my current job are a part of this challenge and thus one can see how the mundane and magical have been brought together by her hands to facilitate my healing, growth, and change.

She is pushing me out of the proverbial nest asking me to prepare to train others and help them as I've been helped, and I'm eager for the new challenge. The hardest part is the split between my teacher and me, at this point, and yet again I know my Lady's hand is at work here as well. Part of the necessity of the split is that I would never otherwise be motivated to move out on my own and take my rightful place and the healing and learning I've undergone would be in part wasted. I suspect in time our paths will merge again, but when the time comes it will be under very different scenarios and with very different roles. This is as it should be, as the Goddess wills it. Truly the chant is correct "She changes everything she touches and everything she touches changes."

Chapter 17: Thru the Darkness to Light

Walking with Hecate has clearly brought much growth and change for me. It has not been easy. She has asked much of me but I would not change it even if I could. Facing our fears, our established beliefs, our perceived limitations are what Hecate is truly all about. She will not ever make the path easy nor will she take your pains from you. Instead she will show you another way to handle them. The part of me that was the frightened, hurting, cut up creature still lives in the recesses of my mind and spirit. Hecate herself can not and will not take her from me, as she told me in that series of journeys thru Dagaz. But today I respect that part of myself. I respect the strength that part of me holds to have endured thru so much. I've learned that I am far more capable and far stronger then I ever could have dreamed. I've learned to visit with that hurting part of myself and hold her close when the road brings me pain and doubt. The road continues to unfold before me and my own healing is far from done. There are still plenty of lessons for me to learn and challenges to meet, but I look forward to them.

Thru all the pains and joys involved the journey has been one of great discovery. Discovery of my past, discovery of my self and the lessons had only just begun. The first part was drawing to a close, the second began with the exploration of the question, Who are you? With the split from my teacher that question would become of profound importance in the second part of my journey. But that is a matter for my next book.

I hope my journey thus far has helped you to see that Hecate is not a deity to be feared, but instead one to be embraced by those ready for change and healing. It is our darkness, our struggles that gives us our strength. She is willing and ready to stand with you thru your own pain and hurt. She is willing to protect and guide you to your own true self. All you have to do is call out to her from your heart and she will answer you. Look and listen well and you will know her answer. Follow her and your life will never be the same. I wish you strength and perseverance on your journey and offer you a key to unlock the gate of its beginning.

Bibliography and Resources

1. Crowfoot Greg. Crossroads, The Path of Hecate. San Diego, Ca. Aventine Press, 2005

2. D'Este Sorita, editor, Hekate, Keys to the Crossroads, London, England: Avalonia 2006

3. Rodrick Timothy. Apprentice to Power. Freedom, Ca. The crossing Press, 2000

   Self injury is a serious condition. **Please** consult your doctor for help. The resources listed here are meant to compliment your doctors assistance and for educational purposes *only*.

4. Conterio Karen, Lader Wendy, Bloom Jennifer. Bodily Harm,. New York, New York Hyperion, 1998

5. Safe Alternatives Program
   www.selfinjury.com 1-800-DON'T-CUT

6. http://www.siari.co.uk

7. Feel free to contact me if you wish to share your walk with Hecate towards healing. I'm not a counselor, or a doctor, merely someone who's been there and knows what it takes to heal. keybearersstriker@gmail.com

www.ingramcontent.com/pod-product-compliance
Lightning Source LLC
Chambersburg PA
CBHW020022050426
42450CB00005B/604